Maria Sibirnaya

Alexander Mardan's plays in the context of mass pop culture

Maria Sibirnaya

Alexander Mardan's plays in the context of mass pop culture

ScienciaScripts

Imprint

Any brand names and product names mentioned in this book are subject to trademark, brand or patent protection and are trademarks or registered trademarks of their respective holders. The use of brand names, product names, common names, trade names, product descriptions etc. even without a particular marking in this work is in no way to be construed to mean that such names may be regarded as unrestricted in respect of trademark and brand protection legislation and could thus be used by anyone.

Cover image: www.ingimage.com

This book is a translation from the original published under ISBN 978-3-659-92355-5.

Publisher:
Sciencia Scripts
is a trademark of
Dodo Books Indian Ocean Ltd. and OmniScriptum S.R.L publishing group

120 High Road, East Finchley, London, N2 9ED, United Kingdom
Str. Armeneasca 28/1, office 1, Chisinau MD-2012, Republic of Moldova, Europe
Managing Directors: Ieva Konstantinova, Victoria Ursu
info@omniscriptum.com

Printed at: see last page
ISBN: 978-620-2-75264-0

CONTENTS

INTRODUCTION

The study of the relationship between dramaturgy and mass culture is an urgent topic due to the noticeable tendencies of mass culture's influence on contemporary public consciousness

Despite the wide popularity of playwright Alexander Mardan both in Russia and Ukraine, as well as in other European countries, no studies in the form of articles and scientific monographs that would fully analyze A. Mardan's plays in the context of mass culture have appeared so far.

All the existing critical works devoted to the works of A. Mardan characterize the various literary and dramaturgical tendencies present in the plays of the playwright, however, have not yet been analyzed those aspects of the plays, which we plan to consider in this paper.

Since the plays of A. Mardan's plays in their stage interpretation, as theatrical productions show, mainly represent a stratum of mass popular culture, we will try to determine how his work fits into the tendencies of existence of the current mass popular drama by analyzing the plays "Anschlag", "Intermission", "The Last Hero" and "Cats and Mice".

The **objectives of** this paper are:

- to trace how stereotypes and clichés of collective consciousness function in the plays of the Odessa playwright, in connection with which a certain mass utopia is created;

- analyze the nature of simulative processes in A. Mardanian's dramas, first of all, at the level of plots, characters' images and speech plan;

- To determine the features of metadramatic techniques used by the author, and on the example of the plays "Anschlag", "Intermission", "The Last Hero" and "Cats and Mice", to analyze, in this regard, the possible ways of interpretation of these plays in the context of mass pop culture.

Alexander Evgenyevich Mardan was born in 1956 in Vladivostok, from where he moved to Odessa with his parents. He graduated from Odessa Mathematics School No. 116, then from Odessa Institute of Marine Engineers. For a long time he worked in the system of the USSR Ministry of Navy. In the early 90's A. Mardan left the naval career, today he is a major businessman and a member of the National Union of Writers of Ukraine. He wrote his first screenplay in 1982, a script for the
television movie in 1985, the first play, "List of Expectations" appeared in 2003 and was published in the almanac "Deribasovskaya - Rishelievskaya" №. 19. To date, written more than twenty original plays and scripts.

In seven years, he has published seven books:

in 2008. - "I'm Different.

in 2009, a collection of plays, "Civil Affairs Day.

in 2010. - "Seven Nights.

in 2011. - The collection "4+2=19",

in 2012. - Ten Plays That Will Shake the World,

in 2013. - Valentine's Night,

In 2015. - "The Story of One Assassination.

Alexander Mardanj's plays have been translated into Ukrainian, Albanian, English, Bulgarian, Italian, Latvian, German, French, Polish, Romanian, Swedish and German. The plays by Alexander Mardanj have been staged in 85 cities of fifteen countries, 156 performances in total.

A.E. Mardan - Laureate of the Gogol Prize 2010. N.V. Gogol 2010. In 2011 for the collection „4+2=19" became a diploma winner of the literary prize named after Yuri Dolgoruky. Yuri Dolgoruky. Laureate of the prize named after. V.I. Dahl 2014. Winner of the prize named after. K.G. Paustovsky 2015. In 2015, A.E. Mardan was awarded the title "Honored Artist of Arts of Ukraine".[1]

A.E. Mardan is one of the most popular playwrights in Ukraine. The audience is not indifferent to the plays of this extraordinary author. There are social and public problems of the plays - funny and sad merged together, you will not immediately realize where the comedy and where the tragedy. Each character has its own hidden drama. A. Mardan's plays should be published in newspapers, because the plots of the plays are so simple and vital and the characters and events are so recognizable.

A. E. Mardan is a master of plot twisting, erudite, aphoristic and witty. According to A. Vinogradova, he "playfully copes with a large volume of multilayered material. A. E. Mardan declared himself as an attentive and biased chronicler - chronicler of his time and the society living in it"[2] .

The playwright sensitively catches the trends that have emerged in society, and promptly transforms them into literature and drama. The author himself says about his work that dramaturgy is not his main activity, but more of a hobby, a passion.

When some playwrights say that modernity is poor in plots, the answer is: „And you go at least to the court, sit there for a couple of days - and there will be enough plots for ten years ahead". Analyzing the wave of new dramaturgy led by some

---

[1] http:// dramaturg. com. ua/index. php/bio
[2] Agnessa Vinogradova, "Was There a Boy?" The magazine "Rainbow", №4, 2011g

scandalous authors,

categorically notes that he does not accept profanity in dramaturgy: When they say that the theater is a temple, let this temple remain at least at the level of vocabulary. And then, apparently, we should remember that the word "ham" in Hebrew is a prohibition. Temple and ham is incompatibility"[34] . The author keeps his audience in the audience by various methods: intrigue in the plot, ambiguous characters, associations with famous classical works, "open" ending, which the audience, and the director too, can interpret in their own way: "the main thing in the theater ... is four components. Cipher. Proportions. Touch. Wave. Like a riddle, form, inclusion and your emotional state.

A.E. Mardan's plays are, in a way, contact lenses that help the reader, the viewer to better see himself, his time, his place among people in our hectic, ambiguous, unpredictable existence.[5]

The art of theater could always be divided into "high" and mass pop culture. In spite of the fact that nowadays theater is associated in the minds of the majority with something always necessarily sublime, the majority of modern plays acquire an exclusively entertaining character, which does not mean a low level of these works at all. A. Mardan's plays also belong to the sphere of modern mass pop culture, which confirms the tendency of our time about the cultural situation in which all types of mass culture exist. It should be noted that mass culture is, according to A. Zakharov and A. Kostina, a form of existence of modern public consciousness.[6]

Considering A. Mardan's plays in the context of mass popular culture and studying the metadramatic techniques used by the author in the plays "Anschlag", "Intermission", "The Last Hero" and "Cats and Mice", we use the following methods:

-        the method of structural analysis, which is used to study all elements and

---

[3]   Remarks on "List". Playwright Alexander Mardan://'gazeta.zn.ua/'CULTURE/remark, na liste dramaturg aleksandr mardan v odes : "In Odessa they speak Russian, but think in Ukrainian^> .:b11pse govoryat po-russki, no dumayut po-ukrainski.html

[4]   Remarks on "Liste". Playwright Alexander Mardan:http://gazeta.zn.ua/CULTURE/remarki na liste dramaturg aleksandr mardan v odes : "In Odessa they speak Russian, but think in Ukrainian."se govoryat po-russki, no dumayut po-ukrainski.html

[5] Agnessa Vinogradova "Was there a Boy?" Rainbow Magazine, No. 4, 2011g

[6]   Zakharov A.V. Traditional culture in modern society [w]: Sociological Studies, 2004, N7, pp. 105-115. Kostina A.V. Mass culture as a phenomenon of postindustrial society, ed.2, M., 2005, p. 352

levels of the poetics of the play as a unified system;

-       elements of the poststructuralist method that help to analyze the plays at the level of such phenomena as performance, metatheatricality, simulacrum, and others;

-       method of intertextual analysis, which is used to comprehend the purpose for which the playwright introduces the intertextual component of Chekhov's and Shakespeare's plays into his own dramas, and to understand how the playwright relates to Russian and world drama, entering into a dialog with the past.

CHAPTER I

1.1. Processes of mass consciousness in mass popular culture.

The term "mass culture" emerged in the 40s of the XX century and became widespread thanks to the works of scientists in different scientific fields: philosophers Jaspers (José Ortega y Gasset *"Revolt of the Masses";* Karl*"Spiritual Situation of Time"*); sociologists (Jean Baudrillard *"Phantoms of Modernity";* P. A. Sorokin *"Man. Civilization.*

Society.") and others. The attitude to mass culture in modern philosophical and cultural thought is not unambiguous. If earlier art was divided into mass and elitist, then in 1960-1970 these concepts were revised within the framework of postmodernism, which removed this opposition for "7 many researchers.

Culture and art, by virtue of their autonomous development, when addressing the masses, are inevitably oriented towards the opportunities and needs of the average average citizen, and thus towards commercial success. For example, the widespread fascination with pop or rock music, simplification and coarsening of literary plots, which we observe, is caused by the scarcity of the inner world of modern man. Most of our contemporaries are unable to accept the polyphonic wealth of images, meanings, symbols, inner experiences and emotions captured in the best examples of classical works.

Mass culture, which exists in parallel and in interrelation with the so-called "high culture", has changed its meaning over the centuries, and the term itself has been redefined in terms of stylistic coloring. In the realistic type of literature, the association of "mass"[7] was associated with tabloidism, bad fiction, kitsch and the image of "low" art in general, as well as drama and literature, in particular.

Today, mass art takes a different form, aimed at the average addressee, who perceives the content of a given image presented in a literary text, cinematography or

---

[7] Theoretical Cultural Studies / Edited by K. E. Razlogov, Moscow: Ros. Institute of Cultural Studies, 2005.

other forms of pop culture as a reflection of the surrounding modern society. The ordinary viewer finds in various types of mass art themes that are close to his everyday life, while high, elitist art deals with issues that are not always clear to him.

Various researchers of postmodern literature have attributed to mass culture such qualities as secondary character and the determining role of the reader[8] . In addition, mass culture proceeds from the adaptation of the values of high culture to mass consciousness, reinterpreting various well-known archetypes of canonical art in a new way, often more understandable for the mass viewer or reader.

Modern mass art increasingly involves the repetition of old motifs rather than the innovation of plots. Popularity is brought by various musical carpets, remakes of film productions, plays, the plot of which becomes stories taken from classic literature and retold anew.

The use of primary ideas that have entered the mass consciousness, the transformation of archetypes into an almost unrecognizable new idea, or the transformation of a classical plot, motif, or image in a new way (often to realize a kind of revolution in consciousness by means of a sharp contrast), has become an artistic technique in the art of the 20th century, in which questions about the relationship between reality and art, great myths and everyday life were repeatedly addressed. In the era of postmodernism, the view of modernity is refracted through the prism of literary and

[9]

the cultural heritage of the past.

Mass culture reflects the perception of the cultural heritage of the past through the stereotypes of mass consciousness. In addition, emerging from the origins of popular culture, mass culture has been most closely connected with everyday life, reflection of the real world and ordinary consciousness. However, mass culture no longer represents a single space, it is complexly structured and includes not only its inherent forms and genres, but also captures the sphere of high culture, includes it in its field, makes it speak its own language. All these phenomena require serious

---

[8] Kostina A. V. Mass culture as a phenomenon of post-industrial society. M., 2003.

comprehension and deep research, without which it is impossible to understand and evaluate the world of contemporary culture.

Unlike high, authorial artistic culture, which, in its essence, aims at comprehending all the problems of human existence, mass culture, touching even the most complex problems of existence, dialectics of feelings, cognition of truth, religion, in the end, simplifies these themes, using stereotypes, simulacra, habitual formulas, clichés, and, thus, draws attention not to the issues of cognition, but to the usual problems of everyday life.[910]

Undoubtedly, the simulacrum is one of the main categories of postmodern aesthetics and philosophy.

Jean Baudrillard (1929-2007).

The concept of simulacrum is associated, first of all, with the name of the prominent French philosopher Jean Baudrillard, according to whom the era of postmodernism is nothing but the era of total simulation. Jean Baudrillard began to use the term "simulacrum" at the end of the 70s. It is in this period that the postmodernist stage of his work opens. In the simulative space of hyperreality, the effect of reality is imitated and exaggerated, creating the impression that all objects, air, and lighting exist in reality.

[9] Shilova E. N. "Metadrama in the work of Caryl Churchill". Ekaterinburg. 2011
[10] Kuznetsova T. F., Lukov V. A., Lukov M. V. "Mass culture and mass belletristics"

The meaning of the concept of "simulacrum" we perceive as an imitation of the nonexistent, repeating the words of Ecclesiastes: *"Simulacrum is not at all what conceals the truth - it is the truth concealing that it does not exist. The simulacrum is the truth. "*In other words, the simulacrum emerges in the process of transformation of the image that reflects reality, gradually masking and distorting reality in order to finally become a symbol that does not hide any reality.[11]

In the scheme of evolution of simulacra, Jean Baudrillard proposes three stages of such development: first-order simulacra acting on the basis of the natural law of value, second-order simulacra - on the basis of the market law of value, and third-order simulacra - on the basis of the structural law of value. Later, in his work "Transparency of Evil" the author of concept develops the scheme and adds the fourth stage of evolution of simulacra - fractal, which corresponds to the "present" state of affairs and is "the most modern".

It is the third and fourth stages of the evolution of simulacra that are of most interest because they are the stages at which the production of moral simulacra begins.

With the advent of the era of simulation, the transformation of reality into hyperreality, the phenomenon of so-called nostalgia appears, the value of the original myths and signs of reality, as well as truth, objectivity and authenticity, "increases". Myths, which have lost their metaphysical origin but retained their regulative mechanisms and function in mass culture, allow, in particular, to organize modern reality.

1.2. Playing simulacra in the dramas of Alexander Mardan in the context of mass popular culture. The context of mass popular culture.

A. Mardan's plays are increasingly gaining mass appeal, as their themes reflect the stereotypes of consciousness and problems of a society living at the crossroads of centuries. The playwright knows the everyday life of his characters in the once great, heroic and long-suffering country, also after its tragic collapse, and uses folk signs and

---

[11] Baudrillard J. "Simulacra and Simulations", translation from French: Pechenkina O.A., 2013 Tula, - 204 pp.

customs. In A. Mardan's plays this material is processed and artistically decorated, but, at the same time, it is conveyed with photographic accuracy and phenomenal observation.

A. Mardan's plays also reflect the human mindset, which for decades was formed under the influence of both the political propaganda of the totalitarian state and a set of different concepts peculiar to the former era. The ongoing destruction and change of the totalitarian regime in the country influenced the transformation of the society's thinking and led to confusion and disappointment.

The new reality brings new ideas into culture, arising as a result of rethinking the stereotypes of the old everyday life, this leads to new interpretations of old motifs, in the process of which there is often a clash of post-totalitarian thinking with outdated but solid ideas of the past.

The attribution of the heroes of A. Mardan's plays to the images present in the consciousness of the masses, the use of established simulacra may also indicate that his work belongs to the genre of mass culture.

Corresponding to similar schemes, A. Mardan's plays repeat the principles of mass fiction, using clichés firmly embedded in the mass consciousness, which the author's irony is aimed at.

In the Soviet and post-Soviet space, there was an attempt to present reality in a utopian image. Soviet propaganda presented the everyday life of the future, i.e. communist life in literature and art, in a peculiar way and aimed at the addressee with the aim of convincing him or her that dreams have partly already been realized. In the post-Soviet years, all memories of the past in literature or art were filled with ideological dogmatism, overplaying and utopianism based on stereotypes associated with totalitarian consciousness. In his plays, A. Mardan tries to show these tendencies, using different perspectives.

---

[1]Uliura G. Conceptualization in Maxim Kurochkin's anti-utopias : individuality and identity [w]: The latest

drama of the turn of the XX-XX1 centuries: the problem of the hero : proceedings of the 4th scientific workshop, April 23-24, 2011, Samara, 2012, p. 49.

In the play "Cats and Mice" there is, as it seems to us, an attempt to restore the broken connection of times, and the whole action turns into a simulacrum of a non-existent reality.

The title of the play "Cats and Mice - A Scandal without Intermission" contains allusions to the meaning of the play. As in other plays by A. Mardan, the title can be interpreted in different ways depending on the general meaning of . Undoubtedly, there is an allusion to the game in which the predator and the victim change places. However, the author leaves it up to the audience to interpret the fact who is the victim and who is the executioner, the predator, the negative hero.

The play "Cat and Mouse" has elements of a talk show, a very popular television program that has recently turned out to be quite a theatrical action with a fictitious reality. In a talk show, what seems to the viewer to be improvisation or suddenly revealed facts is, in fact, nothing more than a precisely thought-out script, which the audience-actors play out in the studio, almost as theater actors play their roles on stage.

The plot of the play "Cats and Mice" attracts the audience's attention with its scandalousness (the word "scandal" is also present in the title). Already at the very beginning the spectator learns about the consequences of the scandal, as the Heroine (a woman in a robe and with a cosmetic mask on her face, yet unknown to the spectator) refuses to give an interview. However, the seemingly ordinary conversation with the Masseuse has the character of an interview with an artist whose life is full of secrets. It is quickly discovered that under the guise of the masseuse turned out to be a journalist Elena, who is trying in this way to collect material for a sensational article about the actress Tamara Leonidovna and her former husband - actor and director, People's Artist of Russia, Jubilee Valentin Ivanovich Platonov, whose relationship between them is shrouded in a scandalous atmosphere after the divorce.

The development of events in such a scandalous way attracts the attention of the viewer and increases the popularity of the play in the same way that glossy magazines and talk shows usually increase their popularity rating. The journalist first pretends to be the daughter of Platonov's first, civilian wife, then reveals the truth, explaining the true motives for her actions by defending her relationship with Tamara's son:

"MASSAGISTIC: [...] If everything works out with Slavik, there will be no article. I'll resign from the editorial office.
What if it doesn't work out?
MASSAGISTIC: Then the article will come out... You have to protect your feelings like you protect your house and your wallet. Otherwise they're worthless."[12]

Elena acts as a judge who makes the guilty think about their actions, turning into a sort of character from an Agatha Christie novel, exposing a family secret - Tamara's adultery with her husband and her sister's husband. The exposure comes in the form of an accusation - another element very typical of crime novels, in which the denouement and information about "who killed" is learned from a super-capable detective. However, the play is not built entirely on the scheme of a thrilling crime story, where all the secrets are revealed towards the end of the work. Throughout the action, different pictures appear before the audience, different versions of the story are intertwined, one scandalous "truth" is replaced by another, reaching its climax in the play's finale.

The image of the actress-Tamara changes throughout the play. From a defenseless victim abandoned by her husband, she turns into the opposite of a victim - an executioner; her whole life turns out to be a game not only on stage, but also in life in front of the closest people. The action (intrigue) takes an unexpected turn at the moment when it turns out that the woman with the cosmetic mask on her face is not Tamara, as the journalist assumed, but her sister Tatiana - the real victim of all events.

The question of simulation, simulation and theatricality often arises throughout the action in various details, trifles and larger elements of the play, which become visible and acquire meaning after the action is over. The subtext of the characters'

---

¹²Mardan A. "Ten plays that will shake the world", Odessa, 2012.

statements allows us to trace the destruction of reality in the post-Soviet space and the transformation of the image of the world and thinking into a blatant simulation. According to J. Baudrillard, simulation differs from mere pretense by the presence of elements of non-existent more real actions, while simulacrum is a representation of the non-existent.[13] The hyperspace of simulation is characterized by the cyclic repetition of events. In such a cycle, according to Jean Baudrillard, there is no definition, which would give rise to numerous or even contradictory interpretations.

In the play Cats and Mice, the characters not only portray other personalities, they live other people's lives and derive a certain benefit from it, but, at times, disappointment as well. Tatiana consciously continues to "play" the role of her sister, an actress, in order to finally discover the truth:

"MASSAGISTIC: You wanted to take the mask off.
It's not time yet."[14]

These seemingly simple words have a double meaning; they may refer not only to the technique of the cosmetic procedure; most likely, this is the moment when she realizes that it is not yet time to take off the mask - both literally and figuratively. The cosmetic mask on the face of the Mistress (Tatiana), whom the journalist has mistaken for Tamara, is one of the allegorical details - clues - with which the play is filled. Allegoricality is also expressed here in the picture of a sheep with wolf's eyes, an image of a creature with the nature of a predator pretending to be a victim. [15]

In the denouement of the play there is a small explanation between the sisters about the conversation between Elena and Tatiana: „And today it so happened..... This girl came, the masseuse, and I was wearing a mask. She said to me: "Tamara Leonidovna, Tamara Leonidovna...". She started to tell me how she went to my, your, of course... performances, how she liked The Seagull... I'm sorry, but I didn't contradict her. I didn't tell her who I was. So I'm sorry, but I was in your shoes for almost an

[13] Baudrillard J. Simulacra and Simulation", translated from French: Pechenkina O.A., 2013 Tula, - 204 pp.
[14] Mardan A. "Ten plays that will shake the world," Odessa, 2012.
[15] Maliutina, N. "Poetics of statements in the plays of Odessa playwrights Anna Jablonska and Alexander Mardan," Rzeszow, 2016, 180s.

hour."[16]

Tatiana recounts what happened, but she omits the essence of her conversation with Elena, instead presenting a very simplified version of it, which she herself seems willing to believe - for the common good. Here we see another example of simulation of the characters, creation of an alternative reality, fear of revealing the truth,
A sacrifice of truth, with both heroines also deceiving themselves.

Nevertheless, paradoxically, it is the theatricality of the heroines' lives that brings them back to reality, to the realization that their lives were full of mixed-up roles. The events presented in the play help Tatiana to gain power over her future life and promote her self-assertion as the director of her own destiny, instead of inertly playing the "role" given from above.[17]

The theatricality of the heroines' lives is not the only association with the theater. As in other plays by A. Mardanian, metadramatic techniques of depicting the theater as a background for the performance and the reincarnation of actresses in different characters are also evident here. The play also has elements of melodrama, a genre of drama that attracts a mass popular audience. The theatricalization of reality, in addition to its semantic meaning, can also acquire here a tinge of author's irony. The cosmetic mask turns out to be a theatrical mask, but at the same time it symbolizes a game, another role in life:

"TAMARA: [...] Tanya, aren't you packed yet? And a mask! We're not going to a carnival. Come on, hurry up." [18]

Carnival is a place where everyone performs in masks. One can trace here an allusion to the fates of Tatiana and Tamara, who confused their roles and found themselves participating in a kind of masquerade.

The play's denouement, based on the model of a melodramatic work, exposes, at

[16] Mardan A. "Ten plays that will shake the world", Odessa, 2012.

[17] Maliutina, N. "Poetics of statements in the plays of Odessa playwrights Anna Jablonska and Aleksandr Mardan," Rzeszow, 2016, 180 s.

[18] Mardan A. "Ten plays that will shake the world", Odessa, 2012.

first glance, the intrigue, but in fact, does not contribute to the completion of the storyline, the play's finale remains open.

Thus, using the discussed techniques, the author achieves the desired result - the play becomes exciting and interesting for the audience even at the end.

1.3. Destruction of the utopia of mass consciousness in the poetics of the play A. Mardan's play "The Last Hero".

A. Mardan's work often reveals the problems inherent in post-Soviet society, such as the destruction of collective utopias due to political changes, provoking an internal conflict between the stable ideas of the past and the new mentality, formed as a defense mechanism in the new reality.

Such problems are seen, in particular, in the play "The Last Hero". The action in the play is organized on the principle of mass, popular television programs, such as reality shows, reflecting the interests and needs of the mass public.

In his plays, A. Mardan often uses elements of game-like situational modeling, principles of role-playing, and elements of scandalous plot. The idea is based on simulacra present in the mass consciousness, the theme is especially directed at the post-Soviet addressee, to whom the mentality typical of the heroes of A. Mardan's plays is most understandable.

The play "The Last Hero" both in its title and subtitle - "reality show" - presents a model of game behavior. The author's purpose in doing so can be considered ironically defamiliarizing, and thus revealing some real analogy between the historical wartime events of 1943 (the defense of Stalingrad) present in the minds of the characters and the mass transmission of the reality show "The Last Hero", popular in our time, which is a constant background throughout the action of the play.

In the plot of the play there is a gradual destruction of the action: along with former traditions, ideals and values, the family and relations between people are collapsing. All this takes place in a house that is falling apart, both literally and figuratively: the community of all the inhabitants disintegrates and they move to different parts of the city, while the house becomes a ruin and is destined for demolition, as all communications are cut off.

The crumbling values are centered in the main space of the play: an apartment, a standard Soviet Khrushchev apartment, in which all the
is reminiscent of Soviet times and reflects the way of life of the generations living in it. Thus, the entire space of the play becomes a simulacrum of the Soviet era.

The picture of the world is presented in great detail by the author in the remarks. Similarly to other plays by A. Mardan, the incidental text clearly depicts the environment of the characters, the place of action of the play is characterized as "a city whose inhabitants speak Russian", the universality of what is happening is emphasized, the events can take place in the city of any post-totalitarian country. In the description of the interior of the apartment, there is also an attempt to draw the reader's attention to the details accepted as standard in the Soviet era: typical Soviet furniture - a "wall" with crystal, a sofa, a carpet on the wall. Apart from the incidental text, allusions to Soviet life are noticeable in the replicas as well as actions of the characters, which, in turn, characterize their mentality, values and approach to change.

The play unfolds in six acts, each of which falls on an official USSR holiday: October Revolution Day (November 7), New Year's Day, Defenders of the Fatherland Day (February 23), International Women's Day (March 8), International Workers' Day (May 1), and Victory Day (May 9). These dates in the modern, post-Soviet reality are celebrated as a tribute to tradition, as well as an expression of beliefs that have not changed due to political changes.

We observe the destruction of Soviet traditions already at the beginning of the play. The day of the October Revolution (November 7) is perceived by the characters more as an occasion for a feast than as a celebration of an event that no longer seems great. In addition, there is a clash between the ideas firmly embedded in the consciousness of the people of the "past era" and the new thinking aimed at modernity, innovation and lack of sentimentality. This juxtaposition of values reflects the dialog between two heroines: Lyudmila, a conservative literature teacher, and Katya,

Lyudmila's daughter, an aspiring actress,

a pragmatic member of the younger generation.

The difference in their characters can be seen in the two women's approach to the family celebration of the now unpopular Revolutionary holiday: Katya is indifferent to the holiday and to meeting her family. Ludmila's conservatism is evident in her fear of change, even the smallest changes, such as hair color or furniture rearrangement. In her mind, everyday routine domestic situations take on a sacralized character, and the ideals under the influence of which she lives do not change depending on her material situation. She appreciates flowers as gifts and, unlike her daughter, is unwilling to exchange them for a more "profitable" form of gratitude. The approach of mother and daughter to the flooding of the apartment by the neighbor above also differs: Katya expresses her distaste for the "abnormal country" in which the tenants do not sue the problematic neighbor and is sarcastic about the fact of friendship between neighbors and the family heroic history of the house itself ("Khrushchevka"), calling it "legends that smell of mothballs.

The elderly neighbor Stalina Petrovna is also a relic of the past - another example of the author's use of recognizable stereotypes of thinking, iconic realities of the Soviet time. Stalina Petrovna is an eyewitness of distant, former times, embodies traditionalism, conservatism, but, at the same time, is introduced to mass culture in the form of television programs, which testifies to the interest of the older generation in pop culture.

The character of the play's protagonist, Victor, brings together all the qualities of a Soviet man, an intellectual who cannot adapt to the new commercial world. This situation shows the next stage of destruction, the transition of one era into another. Victor's character combines the image of a "relic of the past" as an example of a sacralized myth of a real heroic Soviet man, as well as the image of the legendary "last hero". This is how the author's idea is realized: the action in the play develops like the reality show "The Last Hero", a fragment of which is given at the beginning of the play, and Victor turns out to be the "last hero" in this situation, the only "not surrendered" participant in the game into which a rather ordinary situation of our time turns: eviction of tenants from a house to be demolished. The conditions in which the "game" takes place are also similar: in the television program it is a wild jungle, an uninhabited island, while in the play it is a gradually deteriorating apartment building.

The plot of the play is very life-like, as if heard from the mass-media, and in its structure resembles the script of a reality show in which the characters participate. The apartment, on the walls of which the history of generations living in it is imprinted, is gradually being destroyed due to years of exploitation. At the same time, the family problems of the apartment's inhabitants are striking: lack of material resources, disagreement between generations (parents and their daughter), and the fragile marriage of Lyudmila and Victor. The gradual disintegration of the family continues while the characters inertially lead a familiar way of life, observing former traditions as a kind of tribute to the past.

The residential building in which the apartment is located also acquires a sacralized actor. At one time the tenants practically squatted in the house and defended their right to live in it for six months (six months later the residents were issued a warrant); this heroic story is compared in the poetics of the play to the military battle of Stalingrad. This kind of comparison demonstrates both the absurdity of the laws in the former Soviet era of totalitarianism and the attitude of the residents to their house as a relic.

A sudden situation changes the usual course of business and forces a rethinking of real values. The site on which the house stands is destined for a high-budget investment by the firm Atlanta, and the house itself, accordingly, is to be demolished. The residents received a rather favorable offer: for consenting to demolition and voluntary eviction, the firm offered a good monetary compensation and the search for other, better housing. The characters are put before the choice of preferring material or spiritual values. Probably, the author uses here allusions to the motif of "The Cherry Orchard" by A. Chekhov, a comedy that presents the clash of emotions and ideals with the practicality of the new times. In A. Mardan's play, the problem of changing the world and human mentality is also connected with the necessity to part from the place where one's whole life has passed because of material need, and with which one's memory and sentimentality binds one. By analogy with Chekhov's Lyubov Andreyevna, Ludmila is represented as well, for whom the apartment is of supreme value as a memory and a symbol of the past.

Victor presents a very different point of view; it is his behavior in this situation that turns the plot of the play into a "reality" show.
The firm's offer gives the hero an opportunity to get rid of his bad luck, prove his true worth to his surroundings and realize himself. Dreaming of receiving a capital of 200 thousand dollars as a compensation for the cost of the apartment, he wants to open his own business and rehabilitate himself for all past failures.

The model of reality show appears at the moment of Victor's transformation into the last hero - "player" in the situation of gradual agreement of all other tenants with the conditions of the company, and thus, it can be considered that they are eliminated from the game by . Victor stubbornly disagrees with the increasingly large sums of money offered by the representative of the firm and explains his plan to everyone around him. In fact, the meaning of such a fantastic, unthinkable idea is not in material means, but in the self-realization of the hero's personality.

We get to know Victor's character through his behavior, manner of speaking, and from the conversations of others about him. Many unrealized plans, failures, and the constant feeling of being incomplete, superfluous both in the country and the new time, and in his family, which he cannot provide for, cause the hero's despair, pushing him to actions close to madness. However, the dreams are not realized, Victor not only does not find himself as a new, full-fledged person, but is deprived of the little that he had before, remains abandoned by his wife and deprived of hopes for changing the gray, hopeless existence.

In the play's finale, there is a collision of two "collapsed" elements: the house ("Khrushchevka") and Victor's personality, whose name is
The "winner" is perceived as a sign of the author's irony. The ambiguity of the

denouement, the uncertainty of the fate of the "last hero" is a technique that embodies the author's idea and gives the opportunity to interpret the play in different ways. One of the options for interpreting the play can be the idea of the irrevocably gone Soviet era, and with it the death of the man who embodies its ideals.

However, it is necessary to analyze what this kind of depiction of the former epoch really is. All recognizable elements of everyday life: Soviet holidays, feasts with their rituals, fragments of quotations, songs - are a set of stereotypes of everyday behavior. Victor's personality is also an embodiment of mental stereotypes and clichés brought to absurdity. It can be assumed that the character himself (Victor) is a kind of simulacrum of a hero of the Soviet era.

Victor represents a type of former Soviet man who combines all the lost qualities inherent in the people of the past era. One of these qualities is a kind of caricaturized heroism, which does not allow the hero to give up in the struggle to find a decent life and his true identity. The purpose of the author's creation of such a type of hero may be to reject the illusion of Soviet heroism inherent in the mass consciousness.

The impact on the audience is enhanced by the play's musical accompaniment, as each action, in keeping with Soviet holidays, ends with a very famous, sometimes even clangorous piece of music. The last red day of the calendar in the structure of the plot is Victory Day in the play, an allusion to the victory of the tenants of the house many years ago and irony combined with the heroism of Victor, whose defeat occurs just on this day. The popular and multi-generational favorite song "This Victory Day" reinforces the impression of the grotesque nature of the performance.

A. Mardan accurately guesses the audience's mores, showing them in his plays. Everything that attracts the attention of the public in various shows - scandalousness, similarity of plots with ordinary everyday life and, at the same time, unlike ordinary life - is present in A. Mardan's plays, such as "The Last Hero".

The action in his plays is organized and based on certain simulacra, brought to kitsch, which may, in turn, reflect certain literary and cultural traditions. However, questions about the reality of what is happening, the mutation of various spheres of human existence affect the perception of reality, the way people communicate, so one cannot but agree with some researchers of literature, philosophy and sociology, who consider the post-Soviet era as a source of preconditions for changing reality and rethinking traditional values inherent in the mass consciousness of the era of totalitarianism.

Showing different characters and destinies of heroes, revealing the processes going on in modern society, which may be interesting to the general public, A.Mardan uses in his plays different techniques, also metadramatic.

CHAPTER II

2.1. Metadrama and elements of metatheatricality in modern drama. dramaturgy.

The widespread use of metatextual techniques in the literature of the 20th century allows us to talk about the development of the phenomenon of meta-literature. However, metadrama as a phenomenon belonging to a special kind of literature has its own peculiarities.

Metadrama as a theatrical technique has a long history. The notion of "metadrama" appears already in one of JI. Abel's articles of 1963. The new term characterized drama and theater, the problematics of which were addressed to the theater itself[20] . The term "metatheater", proposed by L. Abel, has managed to enter into literary studies, however, it has not yet been assigned a single, universally recognized meaning, and the dramaturgical ways of presenting metatheater as a way of seeing the world and theater have not been fully described. An example of the development of metadramatic techniques in the twentieth century can be considered the plays of B. Brecht, in which there is a direct address of the actor to the audience. Metadrama became one of the main tools of self-reflection of the theater, turning the structure of the theatrical performance into its main character.

Among the distinctive features of 20th century metadrama - autoreflexivity, a complex hierarchy of levels of stage reality, and repetition - are largely determined by the creative findings of L. Pirandello and B. Brecht. Postmodernism increases the degree of metadrama's reflexivity through reference to precedent literary works and their reinterpretation .[21]

In postmodernist metadrama, there is a doubling of reality, which implies

---

[20] Polityko E.H.. "Metadrama in modern theater". Bulletin of Perm University 2010.
[21] Shilova E. N. "Metadrama in the works of Caryl Churchill".Dis.... Cand. philolog. nauk . Ekaterinburg.2011.

metadramatic comments in the course of the plot development, contrasting distribution of roles (roles are performed without taking into account the age and gender of actors, the number of characters does not correspond to the number of artists), compositional repetitions or presentation of parallel variants of the development of events on stage. The metadramatic aspect can manifest itself in a variety of forms - from individual statements of a character and a plot line (P. Calderon, L. Thicke) to a dramatic structure that creates an image of "global theater" (L. Pirandello, M. de Gelderod, T. Stoppard) .[22]

Metadrama can also be realized in the form of "a play within a play" and "a play about a play", as well as in plays about theater. In works characterized by metadramatic and theatricality of space, the theater is emphasized stagey and goes beyond its limits, competing with "real" life in terms of the adequacy of perception of events. There are also "conditionally nominative" lines and comments that lead to the realization of the abstract nature of language. Another element of metatheater is the use of scenery that emphasizes the theatrical conventionality of the action. The use of the plot of a classical work in another, new play is characteristic of metadrama.

The formula "theater in the theater" in each era has been filled with its own meaning. The traditional version of "theater in the theater" is an extended metaphor: the world is a theater. The external drama - life - is opposed to the internal drama
- theater, and the whole text is a metaphorical juxtaposition of them. B. Chupasov considers two main types of metadramatic plays: _~ _ 23 classical and modernist
.

The classical version of metadrama is the representation of the world as a huge theater, according to Shakespeare's maxim "All the world is a theater. In it, women, men are all actors". People in everyday life "play", perform roles sometimes without even realizing it. Being in the theater, they have the

---

[22] Stavitsky A. V. " Metadrama G. Büchner and the problems of its stage realization "Cand. of Arts. St. Petersburg. 2002.

opportunity to observe what is happening on the stage, detaching themselves from it as from an alternative reality.

Modernist dramas, on the other hand, containing the "scene on stage" technique, are intended to show that there are no clear boundaries between art and reality. Modernist theater does not reflect reality, but is an integral part of it. Theater here is not a representation of life, but an element of it. According to the definition of the modern researcher E.N. Polityko, metadrama is a representation of life. Polityko, metadrama is a type of drama that uses the principles of autoreflexion, repetition and playful doubling of reality.

Metadrama combines all cases in which the play manifests the idea embodied by the theater of the constructedness of what happens in it, of the transformation of life into theater and vice versa.

The technique of "theater in the theater" has long attracted the attention of drama researchers. This technique has been written about both on the material of the dramaturgy of W. Shakespeare, J. B. Moliere, A. Chekhov, and contemporary playwrights. One of the most famous examples of metatheatricality is the play by W. Shakespeare. Shakespeare[23][24] "Hamlet", in which the technique of "theater in the theater" is used as an inserted component of the play.

In A. Chekhov's play "The Seagull", each plan of the theatricalized "reality" has its own features: the pathetically melodramatic character of the heroine Nina is revealed in the inconsistency of her monologues with the action and lines of other characters, Nina constantly feels herself as the heroine of the play, which she tries to play not only in an amateur performance, but also in life. Thus, in The Seagull, the metadramatic device can be considered an element of metatheatricality.

According to E. Sokolova, the technique of "theater in theater" is dramaturgical method, which allows us to uncover the very nature of theater, to

---

[23] Chupasov V. B. " Scene on the stage": the problem of poetics and typology. "Dissertation of Candidate of Philological Sciences. Tver State University, 2001

[24] Polityko E.H.. "Metadrama in modern theater", Vestnik Permskogo universitet. 2010.

make it the content of the dramaturgical text and stage performance .[25]

Metadrama, as a genre of dramaturgy, implies emphasized theatricality, doubling of artistic reality, erasure of boundaries between the world of reality and the world of art. The techniques used emphasize the hero's lack of self-identity[26] . The action of a play known to everyone can be transferred to other realities, the time can be changed, for example, the staging of a classic play by W. Shakespeare is carried out in modern reality. Replicas of the characters can be changed and contain reminiscences or allusions from other plays.

All of the techniques presented are involved in the emergence of the
of a certain type of artistic and theatrical thinking, which makes it possible to see how the latest drama manifests the artistic self-consciousness of the time.

2.2. Reception of "theater in the theater" in the play by Alexander Mardan "Anschlag".

Of course, the interpretation of a theatrical work depends on whether it is presented on stage or exists as a text of drama, in written form. The play "Anschlag" is a full-fledged element of both literature and drama.

Analyzing the reception of "theater in the theater" and "scene on the stage" in the play "Anschlag" by A. Mardan. Mardanian's play "Anschlag", we are based on the positions of scholars (E. Sokolova, A. Stawicki, A. Skolasinska, E. Polityko, etc.), who in their works analyzed a number of regularities of the functioning of this technique in plays and distinguish it by its role and by the nature of creating the structure of the action.

Russian dramaturgy has repeatedly addressed the phenomenon of theatricality as a certain component of our life. An example is the dramaturgy of A. Chekhov and his play "The Seagull", in which the problem of man's

---

[25] Sokolova E. B. "Theatrical self-reflection in the dramaturgy of the epoch of modernism" Izvestiya RGPU named after A.I. Herzen, 2007, Vyp № 43-1 / vol. 17, c.316-319

[26] Shilova E. N. "Metadrama in the works of Caryl Churchill". Cand. philolog. sciences . Yekaterinburg. 2011

needlessness appears and the impossibility of his self-realization in the conditions of the late XIX and early XX century is realized.

In a letter (October 1895) A. Chekhov calls "The Seagull" a comedy "in which there are three female roles, six male roles, four acts, a great deal of talk about literature, little action, much love". The same can be said about A. Mardan's play "Anschlag", in which Chekhov's "The Seagull" is the starting point for creating a picture of the world and the poetic atmosphere of the play.

While the classical version of metatheater points to the similarity between the world and the theater, and the modernist technique of "theater in the theater" destroys the boundaries between theater and life, we can see in A. Mardanian's play a combination of these techniques. Mardanja's play is a combination of these techniques.

Reality in the perception of the characters has no unambiguous meaning. Theater, on the other hand, acquires meaning not only as art, but also as an integral element of life. Unlike many plays, where motto is more or less present but has no meaning, the whole concept of action of the play Anschlag is based on the idea of theater. The model according to which the theater functions is revealed to the audience from the beginning to the end. However, "Anschlag" presents theater not only as art or entertainment. Play is not an element of life here, but life itself.

The story presented in the play "Anschlag" is a proof of the presence of theater in our lives. The heroes of the play are actors, representatives of the idea of the world-theater, who live by playing. At the same time, the play raises the problem of the impossibility of cognizing the boundaries between reality and play, and the possibility of influencing life with the help of illusion. Therefore, the play by A. Mardan's play can be interpreted both from the angle of the classical interpretation of the "theater in the theater" technique and from the perspective of the modernist concept.

The play's protagonist Konstantin is the embodiment of the perception of the theater as the only remaining way to escape from the falsity of everyday life, that is, as a way to find the truth he has lost. Konstantin falls in love with Nadezhda, in whom, however, he sees not only a real woman, but also the heroine of The Seagull. In order to win her favor and love, he devises a "performance" in which two people talk to each other. in which two people talk about life, about feelings, about mutual understanding. We see how the main play plays out the "Performance", which can also be considered life.

The actions of the protagonist, who turns to acting as an attempt to change and give his life a different meaning and find love, are interpreted differently by the other characters in the play.

The motives for his action seem different depending on the point of view of different characters. Larisa believes that there is no art in "Performance": "Well, a man and a woman are talking, throwing lines like a ball. And what is the moral? ... Is this theater? It's a talk show"[27] . About the hero, she says that he is "mad with fat". Director Yevgeny Sergeevich believes that Konstantin "entered the theater as in the altar of the temple, behind the iconostasis ... All can not, but he can. Not without reason they say that the theater is a temple, only in the church a man comes to communicate with God, and in the theater - with Man"[28] . Another actress, Anastasia, considers Konstantin's behavior as entertainment of a rich bored businessman who has enough money to fulfill his whims. In her opinion, Konstantin wants to "buy" someone else's love instead of finding his genuine one. In Nadezhda, the woman he has come to love, Konstantin finds no understanding; she is "eternally grateful to him," and only .[29]

Analyzing the play, we can notice that "Performance" reveals the principles not of classical theater, in which action prevails, but of modern theater, the main content of which is the process of creating theatrical illusion. We observe in it the features of performance, which is common in contemporary interpretations of

---

[27] A.Mardan. Ten plays that will shake the world, Odessa, 2012, p. 101.
[28] 28 п-
       1am
[29] A.Mardan. Ten plays that will shake the world, Odessa, 2012, p. 101.

both modernist and new postmodernist plays. Performance is an aesthetic of contemporary cultural consciousness, a technique of interactive communication with the audience in the theater, a way of conducting a dialog with the audience. In the process of performance, the spectator can become part of the action, sometimes without even realizing it.

The ambiguity of Konstantin's behavior, the ambiguous understanding of the motives behind his desire to live on stage and the uncertainty of the play's denouement can be interpreted as a manifestation of the poetics of the play "Anschlag", i.e. as another element of metatheatricality.

At first glance, it seems that in "Anschlag" there are solid analogies with Chekhov's "The Seagull", but, on the other hand, Konstantin's resemblance to Treplev may be a device of the grotesque. During the month when Konstantin visited the theater and watched "The Seagull", he decided to enter the role of Treplev, although, in fact, the similarity of his character to Chekhov's hero is ambiguous.

Konstantin's desire to live by acting could be realized not only on stage, in the "Performance", but also in life, as Konstantin decided to start living an illusion. Having imagined himself to be Treplev, he behaves in such a way as to appear to be him all the time.

E.N. Polityko in her work "Metadrama in Modern Theater" draws attention to the cognate connection between metadrama and metaliterature, pointing to the ability to develop a new level of self-knowledge in drama. She examines the nature of metadrama and draws attention to the use of techniques in drama such as remarks through which the author can express his or her own view of the play .[30]

A. Mardan uses remarks as a technique necessary for a certain interpretation of his work. The very title of the play "Anschlag" by A. Mardan means not only what we are accustomed to understand in everyday life - the lack of free seats in the theater hall, but also other interpretations of this word: a blow, an attempt, an

---

[30] Polityko E.H.. "Metadrama in modern theater". Bulletin of Perm University. 2010.

estimate, an estimate, a calculation, a game of wand. This author's technique of multivalent interpretation of the title already from the very beginning of the play indicates the possibility of ambiguous interpretation of the action, conflicts, and characters.

The main character of the play, Konstantin Georgievich Borisov, is a disillusioned rich businessman who decides to turn to the theater in order to find himself. For him, the theater represents a kind of salvation, a kind of religion. The theater evokes in him associations with the feeling of "home", childhood memories and a time when the world did not seem so sad and artificial.

Konstantin realizes the pretence of everyday life. After all, everything he does is a learned, machine-like action, little different from the play of puppets - marionettes. He is forced to fulfill the laws of society, to observe decency, as it is required of him by others, and as his social status as a businessman requires. However, this inert life does not give him happiness. Konstantin tries to live on stage every night in order to make sense of his inner world, emotions, and to find himself. "Everyone lives by playing, but only actors, by playing, live"[31] - apparently, these words inspire and constitute the meaning of the main character's life. In search of truth, he turns to the theater, to the game, because, in his opinion, the feelings played on stage are genuine.

The element of vitality of the play "Performance", played by businessman-entrepreneur Konstantin, is what attracts the audience most of all and leads to a full house. According to the head of the theater, "a person comes to the theater to communicate with a person", i.e. watching what is happening on stage turns into a psychotherapy session. The success of "Performance" is explained by the human desire to observe the feelings of others in order to analyze one's own state of mind.

About "The Seagull" A. Chekhov said that there is little action in it, but a lot of talk about love, "Performance", as a play within a play or a theater within a theater, and is a conversation about love or an attempt to live a true life in the

---

[31] Mardan A.. Ten plays that will shake the world, Odessa, 2012, p. 101.

process of conversations between two loving people. What happens on stage intrigues the audience in the way that a talk-show or simple life stories and gossip usually intrigues. Interpreting the action, each in his own way, the viewer finds something that relates to himself.

The Performance also contains allusions to Chekhov's The Seagull, or rather, we can speak of an alternative action. In The Seagull, the characters live in a state of misunderstanding of themselves and others. The tragic end comes because of unrequited love, focus on their inner world, and inattention to others.

The "performance" is a very different, optimistic, but at the same time, plausible reality. The characters come to mutual understanding by communicating together - dialog is the path to happiness. "Performance" also reveals the dream inherent in both Constantine and all the audience, who, watching what is happening, experience catharsis.

Another explanation of Konstantin's action may be the hero's desire to realize his subconscious dream of realizing his need for theatricality. According to N. Evreinov: "A man is theatrical because he strives to be or seem something that is not himself". At the heart of theatricality - "the instinct of transformation", "the joy of self-change", "the first motto of theatricality - not to be yourself"[32] . The theatricality of behavior brings a kind of satisfaction to a person: he feels the power of his own influence on others and as if revels in his own play or affective self-expression.

In this case, the hero, using the play of his authorship, wants to simultaneously live the best, "ideal" life of his dreams and "open his soul" in front of the audience. He wants to achieve self-realization in the process of theatricalizing himself, his " I " .[33]

Following the embodiment of his ideas into reality, the hero consciously changes his real life into an illusion and lives it in the form of a theatrical

---

[32] Evreinov N. "Theater as such. Justification of theatricality in the sense of the positive beginning of stage art in life", Izd.2-nd, supplement. M., Vremya, 1923.
[33] Khalizev V.E. "Drama as a phenomenon of art" Art. Moscow. 1978.

performance. Konstantin is the embodiment of a man who has swapped the places of pretense and reality. However, failing to find understanding in Hope ("There is hope, but no hope"), Konstantin makes the only choice left to him, he chooses death, as he cannot return to reality, where the "death of desires" has already occurred .[34]

The poetics of A. Mardan's play contains the ambiguity of interpretation of the denouement. The sad ending, the disappearance of the protagonist can be seen not only as a suicide, but also as a death in connection with another attempt on the businessman. Another interpretation can also be Konstantin's desire to get away to "his island", and some viewers will understand it not in a figurative but in a literal sense.

The intrigue in the denouement is a tribute to the audience, which gets to choose its own ending to the play. In this case, it can be seen as an element of reality in a world full of lies.

Thus, we see in the play "Anschlag" the manifestation of several metadramatic techniques, various elements of the "theater-in-theater" technique, those that are usually personified with metatheater (for example, acting out the play in the play), but also a method ov more innovative. The metadramatism of the play "Anschlag", taking features of both classical and modernist versions of this technique, is visible in the plot of the play, in various allusions and analogies to other, classical plays and in the discourse on the problems inherent in the theater. By combining all these components, the play "Anschlag" provides an excellent opportunity to illustrate the various properties of both metatheater and the art of theater in general.

A. Mardan's mass popularity is based on his dramas, which are staged in the theaters of many post-Soviet countries, as well as translated into foreign languages. However, Alexander Mardan in his work does not stop at drama, but expresses himself also in prose.

---

[34] Mardan A. "Anschlag. (History of one attempt)." Odessa. 2010.

An interesting fact is that among the stories and novellas of the playwright noticeably stand out works that are a kind of repetition of the plots of the plays. So far there have appeared under the novella: "The Story of One Assassination", "The Last Hero" and „Valentine's Night".

All three stories at first glance repeat the story that is conveyed in the dramas, but, in fact, there are also some differences that change, if not the text, then its possible interp ertation.

Thus, "The Story of One Assassination" is transferred to prose play, "Anschlag" with the subtitle, "The Story of One Assassination".

While the stage adaptation should adhere to the text of the play, and the action is limited to the stage and theatrical opportunities, the director's vision of the play, in the story we can observe the opposite phenomenon - the text is noticeably expanded, the action takes place in different places, the reader is presented with the inner world of the characters, the author's interpretation of the characters and motives for their actions is also manifested.

One of the main differences in the plot is an additional character, which in the play, in turn, is only mentioned by the protagonist. This is Gleb, a journalist with whom Nadezhda "managed" to get acquainted, and whose affair with him finally led the protagonist Konstantin to his death. The death of the protagonist, which was hinted at in the play, leaves not the slightest doubt in The Story of One Assassination.

The atmosphere of the story is filled with details that are absent in the play, which allow the reader to better recognize the realities of what is happening, however, the author's comments in their own way explain the reasons for the characters' actions, their relationships and life decisions, as well as the results of these decisions, almost without giving the reader the opportunity to individually comprehend what is happening.

The story "The Story of One Assassination" is full of the author's reasoning about the theater. Comparing the world of reality and illusion in the behavior of the characters, the author reveals the mechanisms of influence of theater, theatricality and fiction on human outlook and fate.

Despite the fact that the story is a prose work, it has the character of metatheatricality because of the theme of theater present everywhere, the story also shows a fragment of "Performance" staged on the small stage of the theater, i.e. another element of metatheatricality is used.

Thinking about why A. Mardan transfers the plots of plays into prose, we come to the conclusion that it is a matter of greater popularity of work. The story has a larger circulation, gives the author a greater opportunity to express himself and have an impact on the minds of readers than a play.

One reason may be the author's desire to try to enter into a dialog with those who do not attend the theater and prefer reading novels to reading plays. Another may be the playwright's desire to express his or her own ideas about the characters, to interpret his or her own plot, which in the process of staging a play is a script worked out and presented by the director and actors.

2.2. Factors of influence of Chekhov's text on the poetics of plays A. Mardan's plays "Intermission" and "Anschlag".

In this subsection we want to address the problem of the attitude to the classical tradition, its peculiar dictate, which is overcome in various ways by contemporary theater dramaturgy.

Many modern plays are created on the basis of precedent texts, and quite often a completely new original author's text is created on the basis of a classical work. A number of researchers of modern dramaturgy in their works consider the problem of the reception of classical theatrical works in the plays of contemporary authors. Thus, O. Zhurcheva in her article *"Receptive Strategies* in *Modern Dramaturgy"* draws attention to the phenomenon of creative reception in modern dramaturgy and notes that the contemporary situation in dramaturgy is similar, perhaps, only to the equally massive experience of the 1920s. Perhaps dramaturgy in the twentieth century and now the twenty-first century.

It becomes the leading genus when it is necessary to master, to understand the new social 35 reality .

Classical works are a kind of reference point, a point of reference, a precedent text that organizes the text of contemporary plays. The undisputed leader in the frequency of attribution in contemporary Russian plays is A. Chekhov's theater .[35]

The text of Chekhov's dramas appears as "a kind of aesthetic (...) ideological 'archetype' present in the consciousness of both the mass audience and the newest playwrights"[36] . This was the beginning of a dialog a of contemporary playwrights with A. Chekhov through the transformation of his ideas and works, firmly embedded in the consciousness of modern man. Modern playwrights turn to "alien" plot and "alien" word to ostracize the known models of the works of the school program and to extract some present-day meaning in them .[3738]

Thus, the playwright who exists within the framework of another's plot, quotation, and dramaturgical scheme becomes the very "model of the imaginary reader" that Umberto Eco wrote about, who "will be able to interpret perceived expressions in exactly the same " " „39
in the spirit in which the writer created them" .

In A. Mardan's plays "Intermission" and "Anschlag", even at first glance, one can clearly notice allusions to Chekhov's drama, repetition of motifs, intertwining of the names of the characters of Chekhov's plays, however, the

---

[35] Sergeeva E., Maslenkova N., "Dialogue with the classics as a means of building conflict in modern literature". 2009.

[36] Zhurcheva O.V. " Prescriptive strategies in the newest drama" [w]: The newest drama of the turn of the XX-XX1 centuries: the problem of the author, prescriptive strategies, the vocabulary of the newest drama. Materials of scientific and practical seminars, Samara, 2009, p.26-27.

[37] Zhurcheva O.V. " Prescriptive strategies in the newest drama" [w]: The newest drama of the turn of the XX-XX1 centuries: the problem of the author, prescriptive strategies, the vocabulary of the newest drama. Materials of scientific and practical seminars, Samara, 2009, p.26-27.

[38] *Eco, W.* "The Role of the Reader. A study on the semiotics of text" / U. Eco. Per. from English and Italian.

C. Serebryanyi, St. Petersburg, 2005.

problems inherent in Chekhov's works are presented in a new way.

The play "Intermission" in its form very noticeably, almost compulsively echoes Chekhov's comedy "Three Sisters", recognized by researchers as a tragicomedy. This similarity begins with the names of the characters and is manifested in the staging of the play, which is staged throughout almost the entire action of "Intermission".

All the events of the play are theatricalized: the life of the actors, who transfer life on stage to reality and vice versa, is presented; the specifics of the actors' profession, shown "from behind the scenes" and the problematics of the latest dramaturgy and directing. When considering the nature of intertext in A. Mardan's plays, attention is drawn to its introduction not only in the main text, but also in the incidental text, which allows the reader to discover the names of the heroines of "Three Sisters". A. Mardan borrows the popular postmodernist technique of creating a text within a text.

In the poetics of the play there is a clash between a traditional approach to drama and innovative views on the nature and aesthetics of theater art. The play also contains certain phrases from Chekhov's plays, which are firmly embedded in the mass consciousness of the audience, used to emphasize the connection with Chekhov's text.

In another play by A. Mardan - "Anschlag" The text of Chekhov's "The Seagull" is the basis for creating a picture of the world and the poetic atmosphere of this play. The action also takes place in the theater, and the essence of the meaning of the main character Konstantin's life (an allusion to Konstantin Treplev in "The Seagull") is to play both in front of himself and the real audience. The behavior of the heroes suggests the characters of Chekhov's play because of similar actions (the suicide of the Chekhov hero and the guilt of the woman he was in love with), taking place against the background of contemporary events or simply because of the desire to imitate. [39]

---

[40] Makarova V.V. " Chekhov's intertext in the plays of neorealists of 2000-ies: constructive comprehension of the classics", Vestnik of Buryat State University, Vyp. 10, Ulan-Ude, 2012., pp. 135-

In the play "Anschlag" one can notice a feeling of similarity between Konstantin and Treplev, a kind of repetition of Chekhov's "The Seagull" metadramatism. In "Intermission" such an analogy arises in connection with another Chekhov play - , "Three Sisters": the names of the characters are repeated, during the whole action Chekhov's play is staged several times.

The "influence" of the poetics of A. Chekhov's plays on A. Mardan's plays is noticeable from the first glance. Various researchers pay attention to the strategy used by the author to create an impression of repetition, analogy with the precedent text.[40] These may be puns, names of characters, borrowed lines of characters and language play. A number of researchers argue that all allusions to Chekhov's drama, so vividly expressed in A. Mardan's plays, are nothing but superficial allusions, hackneyed phrases and motifs, clichés - everything that is very easily perceived by any viewer or reader with a minimal secondary education.

Thus, Chekhov's motifs in A. Mardan's plays cannot be regarded as an expression of a new author's idea, but as a classic text easily recognizable in a play by a modern playwright. Such a technique can draw attention to itself, and the spectator will feel himself as someone more educated and, therefore, better than ordinary marginalized individuals. All the "Chekhovian inserts" in Mardan's plays serve precisely to attract this kind of snobbish-intellectual audience.

Another idea draws attention to itself is a kind of snobbish pretensions of the characters (Konstantin, Pavel Bogomolov), who want to transform their life into a more interesting, refined one through the art of theater. Despite the fact that theatricality of behavior is peculiar to all people, the desire to swap illusion and reality can bring neither success, nor happiness, nor an answer about the meaning of one's existence.

140.

[40] Makarov A. B. "Metatheater under the sign of Chekhov (on the material of plays by V. Levanov, O. Bogayev, A. Mardan)", Vestnik Baltic Federal University named after I. Kant, Vyp. 8, Kaliningrad, 2013, pp. 162-168.

Analyzing the reasons for the presence of Chekhov motifs in A. Mardan's plays in such a large number, we can say that nowadays the prevailing tendency is to "remake" classics in a new, modern way, or to stage well-known plays once again in order to rethink their existence through classics. The remake is thus used to attract as many spectators as possible, to gain mass popularity. Apparently, the strategy can also be interpreted in a similar way

A. Mardan, i.e. to assume that everything "Chekhovian" in his plays is a way to attract the attention of the public and, using classical motifs, to say something of his own.

The "Intermission" draws attention to the heroines' loss of the meaning of Chekhov's phrases due to their frequent repetition at rehearsals; the world of Chekhov's classics becomes colorless in their performance, like worn-out costumes. In the finale, however, Chekhov's text brings the actresses closer together, the phrases from The Three Sisters that they utter from the stage become their own, and their performance, for the first time in many years, inspires.

Thus, one can observe the inner change of the heroines through their reinterpretation of Chekhov's text. However, the thought comes to mind: is there really an influence of Chekhov's text on A. Mardan's plays in the form we are used to noticing in mass modern culture: or is it a question of bringing some element of Chekhov's work closer to the consciousness of the average viewer, or can an alternative story of "what would happen if..." be presented?

Despite the fact that, at first glance, the play "Intermission" seems to be based entirely on the precedent text of A. Chekhov's drama "Three Sisters", this similarity does not fully determine the interpretation of the play and its philosophical meaning. All the "Chekhovian clichés" that appear in "Intermission" can be seen not as an attempt to retell "Three Sisters" anew, but as a manifestation of the author's original thought.

The irony of the author's thought speaks of the exhaustion of original motifs in the text and the impossibility of further interpretations of Chekhov's texts. The attempt to extract new ideas from a rather frequently interpreted text, the constant striving to show innovation in art testify to the crisis of the director's theater, as some researchers have written about it.

The play "Anschlag" by A. Mardan is filled with the atmosphere, the space of the theater, theater performances, rehearsals and conversations about human existence in the theater. Chekhov's "The Seagull" may seem to be the basis of the plot of the play and, as in many other plays of the playwright, Chekhov's quotations are recognized in the poetics. The main similarity with "The Seagull" arises from - because of the hero Konstantin, who with his behavior persistently repeats the attempts of Konstantin Treplev to express himself through theatrical art, often in its unconventional form. Just as in The Seagull Nina Zarechnaya "kills" Treplev with her confession, A. Mardan's heroine Nadezhda is the cause of Konstantin's disappearance. The unsaid nature of the denouement makes it possible to interpret it ambiguously. However, all this is rather an imitation of the analogy with The Seagull, the excess of Chekhov's text turns Anschlag into a parody of imitation of classical authors.

The author of the play, apparently, did not intend to transpose Treplev's image into a modern manner; despite other realities and times, Treplev remains the same. The businessman Konstantin does not appear here as a "new Treplev" who has changed his actions and judgments. The play emphasizes not Konstantin's similarity to Treplev, but his absurd imitation of him, even to the point of committing suicide because of a woman.

Konstantin is also an example of an extreme passion for theater and a misinterpretation of the influence of theater on life. In mass popular culture, characters from precedent texts are often used to express such ideas.

The play is a kind of destruction of the classical forms of Chekhov's text by the heroes of Anshlag, an attempt to extract new ideas from a rather frequently interpreted text, and a constant striving to show innovation in art. Stylization, metatextualization, deconstruction and reinterpretations in the form of remake are the processes through which a kind of dialogue with the classics is carried out. In his plays, the playwright uses almost all of these techniques.

The plays under consideration - "Anschlag" and "Intermission" - contain allusions to various innovative theatrical interpretations of A. Chekhov's canonical drama. Chekhov. The poetics of the text traces the playwright's desire to ironize the countless productions of A. Chekhov's plays, which are oriented only to surprise or eupatize the audience.

It is possible that all the action in Mardan's plays is centered around the very process of Chekhov's text influencing the consciousness of people, actors and directors. The plot of the plays concentrates on one problem: the impossibility to escape from the influence of the authority of Chekhov's theater. In the play "Intermission", such "victims of Chekhov's influence" are the actresses of the provincial theater, who through the lines of Chekhov's heroines express their own emotions. In Anschlag, Konstantin falls under the influence of Chekhov's theater and is swallowed up by the space of Chekhov's The Seagull

The author touches upon the impossibility of leaving Chekhov's world, which is inherent in the consciousness of his characters. The influence of Chekhov's text often deprives the characters in A. Mardan's plays of the ability to make their own decisions. In both plays, there is no complete return to precedent texts and the development of Chekhov's thoughts; neither is there a presentation of classical motifs in an innovative, revolutionary form. The development of the action represents the characters' attempt to break free from the influence of the authority of Chekhov's theater, and the characters' return to the precedent text is facilitated by their desire to change their lives.

CONCLUSION

Having analyzed the work of Alexander Mardan, we came to the conclusion that his works are of a mass character.

Various factors of mass pop culture influence aspects of A. Mardyan's work in general, and the plays in question, "Anschlag", "Intermission", "The Last Hero", "Cats and Mice", in particular. The plays contain elements characteristic of drama in the context of mass culture: melodramatism, criminal motifs, the construction of action by analogy with television programs such as reality shows, talk shows, elements of scandalous plot or the use of motifs of classical works to attract the attention of the public.

The audience's perception of plays depends to a greater extent on the stage interpretation of the work. The intrigue in the denouement is a tribute to the audience, which is given the opportunity to guess how the action will end; the spectator also has the opportunity to draw his or her own conclusions. In this case, it can be seen as an element of reality in a world full of lies. By juxtaposing the world of reality and illusion in the behavior of the characters, the author proposes to understand the nature of the impact and influence of theater, theatricality and fiction on human outlook and destiny.

Another element of metadramatism, present in A. Mardan's plays, is the peculiar dialog with the classical plots of A. Chekhov in most of the works. Chekhov. However, such an example of intertextuality should be considered not as a remake, but as an original work, in which the playwright does not limit himself to the repetition of well-known motifs of the classics, but only uses their themes to create the background of the play, in which he expresses his own ideas and views on reality.

The author touches upon the impossibility of leaving the Chekhovian world inherent in the consciousness of his characters; the influence of the Chekhovian text often deprives the characters of A. Mardan's plays of the opportunity to make their own decisions, and the return of the characters to the precedent text occurs only as a result of an alternative, individual desire of the characters to change their lives.

What at first glance appears to be a classic Chekhov story presented in the realities of another country and era is actually the author's irony directed at current trends in popular culture and theater.

A certain tendency should be noted in the perception of plays by the public. A. Mardan's plays are very popular for stage staging, but there is no great demand for reading. This fact can be explained by the inaccessibility of published books with A. Mardan's plays, which is a sign of treating the playwright's work in the context of mass culture: the plays are aimed, rather, at theatrical staging than at their perception in the literary format of a book. Perhaps that is why the author also turns to prose, and the novels "The Story of One Assassination" and "The Last Hero" appear, in which the plot of the plays is repeated. The novellas allow the author to express his view on the events, and should also attract an additional circle of readers, which will add mass popularity to the author.

A. Mardan's plays seem to acquire a mass character, as their themes reflect the stereotypes of consciousness and problems of the society living at the crossroads of centuries. All of A. Mardan's plays are characterized by the presence of elements of utopia of mass consciousness, which is manifested in various stamps in the thinking of the characters. The attribution of the heroes of A. Mardan's plays to the images present in the consciousness of the masses, the use of clichés and simulacra, defining the realities of everyday life and the social status of heroes, can also indicate that his work belongs to the genre of mass culture.

We notice the presence of the Author in the statements of various characters, as well as in the remarque text of the works, which gives both the reader and the viewer of the plays a sense of nostalgia for the past. All this suggests that the author of the plays represents the consciousness of the Soviet era, as evidenced by the theme of the collision of the Soviet mentality with the modern post-Soviet reality and the nostalgia for the Soviet time inherent in the characters of the plays.

The general theme of A. Mardan's plays is characterized by universality; there is no precise definition of the place of action of the plays, except for the author's comment that the characters live in a Russian-speaking city. We find no information either about a specific city or about the country in which the events develop, which allows us to think about the author's possible goal of presenting a plot that could take place in any post-Soviet republic.

Such universal character of the plays leads to the increasing popularity of the author and more and more frequent productions of his works, as the problematics of the plots creates many opportunities for different stage interpretation and individual comprehension.

Having considered the elements of the author's dramaturgy, such as plot, character of action, remarks, images of characters, we come to the conclusion that his plays are intended for a wide range of spectators and can be perceived depending on the way of stage interpretation, the horizon of expectations of the recipient, the context, which is determined both by the social situation and the director's tasks. It seems more convincing to read the playwright's plays in the context of popular culture, which is acquiring more and more weighty significance. Today, its functions and tasks are changing; it is called not only to entertain the public, but also to make them think about the pressing issues of our world and existence.

BIBLIOGRAPHY

1. Baudrillard J. "Simulacra and Simulations", translation from French: Pechenkina O.A., Tula, 2013, - 204 pp.
2. Vinogradova A. "Was there a boy?" Journal "Raduga", № 4, Kiev, 2011.
3. Evreinov N. "Theater as such. Justification of theatricality in the sense of the positive beginning of stage art in life". Ed. 2nd, supplement, M., Vremya, 1923.
4. Zhurcheva O.V. "Prescriptive strategies in the latest drama" [w]: "The newest drama of the turn of the XX-XXX1 centuries: the problem of the author, receptive strategies, vocabulary of the newest drama", Materials of scientific and practical seminars, Samara, 2009, pp. 26-27.
5. Zhurcheva T.V. "Receptive nature of "new drama" as a challenge to the director's theater at the end of the twentieth century" [w]: "The newest drama of the turn of the XX-XX1 centuries: the problem of the author, receptive strategies, the vocabulary of the newest drama". Materials of scientific and practical seminars, Samara, 2011, pp. 72-79.
6. Zakharov A.V. "Traditional culture in modern society" [w]: "Sociological Studies", No. 7, 2004, pp. 105-115.
7. Kostina A. B. "Mass culture as a phenomenon of post-industrial society", ed. 2, M., 2005, - 352 p.
8. Kuznetsova T.F., Lukov V.A., Lukov M.V. "Mass culture and mass belletristics"^]: "Knowledge. Understanding. Mindfulness", No. 4, M., 2008.
9. Makarov A.V. "Metatheater under the sign of Chekhov (on the material of plays by V. Levanov,
10.O. Bogayeva, A. Mardanya)", Vestnik of the I. Kant Baltic Federal University, Vyp. 8, Kaliningrad, 2013, pp. 162-168.
11.Makarova V.V. "Chekhov intertext in the plays of neorealists of 2000-ies:

constructive comprehension of the classics", Vestnik Buryatskogo State University, Vyp. 10, Ulan-Ude, 2012, pp. 135-140.

12.Maliutina, N. "Poetics of statements in the plays of Odessa playwrights Anna Jablonska and Aleksandr Mardan," Rzeszow, 2016, 180 s.

13.Mardan A. "Anschlag. (History of one attempt)." Odessa, 2010.

14.Mardan A. "Ten plays that will shake the world", Odessa, 2012, 101 p.

15.Polityko E.H.. "Metadrama in modern theater (to the production of the

16.problems)". Bulletin of Perm University. Vyp. 5(11),

17.Russian and Foreign Philology, Perm, 2010. p. p. 167-174.

18.Sergeeva E., Maslenkova N., "Dialogue with the classics as a means of building conflict in modern literature" [w]: "Newest drama of the turn of the XX-XXI centuries: the problem of conflict", Samara, Izd--vo "Univers Group", 2009.

19.Sokolova EH. "Theatrical self-reflection in the dramaturgy of the epoch of modernism. Metadrama", Izvestiya RGPU named after A.I. Herzen, Vyp № 431 / vol. 17, M., 2007.

20.Stavitsky A.V. " G. Büchner's metadrama and the problems of its stage realization " Dissertation.... Cand. phil. sciences, 17.00.01. - philolog. sciences, art. lit. of Germany, St. Petersburg, 2012. - 210 c.

21.M. F. Sirazetdinova, "Simulacrum as a means of consciousness manipulation", Young Scientist," No. 2, 2015, pp. 653-655.

22., Deoretical culturology" Edited by K.E. Razlogov, Moscow: Ros. inst. of culturology, 2005.

23. Uliura G. "Conceptualization in Maxim Kurochkin's dystopias : individuality and identity" [w]: "Newest drama of the turn of XXXXI centuries: the problem of the hero", materials of the 4th scientific-practical seminar, Samara, 2012, p. 49.

24.Chupasov V.B. "Scene on Stage: the Problem of Poetics and Typology."

Dissertation of Candidate of Philological Sciences, Tver State University, 2001.

25. Khalizev V.E. "Drama as a phenomenon of art" Art, M., 1978.

26. Shilova E. N. "Metadrama in the work of Caryl Churchill: specificity and dynamics": monograph. - LAP Lambert Academic Publishing, Germany, 2012, 271 p.

27. Eco *W*. "The Role of the Reader. A study on the semiotics of text", translation from English and Italian:. Silver S., St. Petersburg, 2005.

Internet Resources:

28. http://dramaturg.com.ua/index.php/bio(A.E.Mardan. Biography)

29. http ://gazeta. zn. ua/CULTURE/remarks na liste dramaturg aleks andr marda

30. n v odesse govoryat po-russki,no dumayut po-ukrainski.html (Remarks on "List". Playwright Alexander Mardan: "In Odessa they speak Russian, but think in Ukrainian").

Printed by Books on Demand GmbH, Norderstedt / Germany